Deep Sleep Meditation

Ultimate Relaxation Techniques to Quiet Your Mind and Fall Asleep Instantly

Written By

Guided Meditation Therapy

© Copyright 2019 - Guided Meditation Therapy

All rights reserved.

The content contained within this book may not be reproduced, duplicated or transmitted without direct written permission from the author or the publisher.

Under no circumstances will any blame or legal responsibility be held against the publisher, or author, for any damages, reparation, or monetary loss due to the information contained within this book, either directly or indirectly.

Legal Notice:

This book is copyright protected. It is only for personal use. You cannot amend, distribute, sell, use, quote or paraphrase any part, or the content within this book, without the consent of the author or publisher.

Disclaimer Notice:

Deep Sleep Meditation

Please note the information contained within this document is for educational and entertainment purposes only. All effort has been executed to present accurate, up to date, reliable, complete information. No warranties of any kind are declared or implied. Readers acknowledge that the author is not engaging in the rendering of legal, financial, medical or professional advice. The content within this book has been derived from various sources. Please consult a licensed professional before attempting any techniques outlined in this book.

By reading this document, the reader agrees that under no circumstances is the author responsible for any losses, direct or indirect, that are incurred as a result of the use of information contained within this document, including, but not limited to, errors, omissions, or inaccuracies.

Table of Contents

INTRODUCTION 5

CHAPTER 1 – MEDITATION FOR RELAXATION 7

CHAPTER 2 – OVERCOMING TRAUMA, ANXIETY, AND DEPRESSION MEDITATION 25

CHAPTER 3 – MEDITATION TO QUIET YOUR MIND 45

CHAPTER 4 – MEDITATION TO FALL ASLEEP INSTANTLY 63

CONCLUSION 72

Introduction

Sleep is an important part of our life but falling asleep can be incredibly difficult. One of the best methods that you can use in order to get more relaxation and a deeper night's sleep is the use of meditation. Throughout this set of guided meditations, we have provided you with tools and mindset exercises to get into the right state of mind for you to be able to hopefully drift asleep. Once you do fall asleep, you might notice that you wake up frequently throughout the night. This could be because you are not getting the right deep sleep. Before we even go to bed, we have to make sure that we are becoming more relaxed. Your relaxation period can't just be the moment that you get into bed, it should start before that. These mindset exercises are going to help keep you in the place needed to get a better night's sleep.

Make sure when you do these meditations that you are in a place that it is okay to fall asleep. You will never want to do this while you are driving a car or doing anything else that requires your attention.

If you do, the meditation won't be as effective, and if it does work, then you might fall asleep. You have to ensure that you're going to be in a safe and comfortable place to fully feel the benefit of all these meditations.

Ensure that you sit somewhere comfortable and focus on your breathing. Keep an open mind and get ready to heal from the inside out.

Chapter 1 – Meditation for Relaxation

Meditation is going to be a great tool that you can use for relaxation. Before crawling under the covers and closing your eyes, you should be calming down your mind. You'll be surprised at how difficult it can be to stay asleep when you are experiencing so much anxiety. In this meditation, we are going to help you understand the anxieties that keep you awake. This meditation will have some affirmations and other helpful tips to make it easier for you to let go of the things that cause you so much anxiety.

Relaxation Meditation for Healthy Sleep

Getting sleep isn't always the hard part. A lot of the times the challenging part comes when we have to actually fall asleep. Falling asleep can be so challenging because we let thoughts running through our mind keep us awake and disturb out rest, even after we have fallen asleep. These thoughts can make it difficult to get deep, restful sleep. You might wake up frequently throughout the night, sometimes in a cold sweat. Or perhaps other times with tears already streaming down your face.

The reason that we can struggle to find deep sleep is because of the anxiety and inability to relax that we experience right before bed. This meditation should be done as you are about to drift away to sleep. Make sure that you are in bed comfortable with no distractions around whatsoever. Your phone should be put far away from you, and you should not be planning on using it after you've completed this meditation. You have gone through all of your processes of getting ready for bed, such as brushing your teeth or hair and getting into pajamas. It is time now for you to fully immerse yourself in your bed. Let yourself stretch out underneath the covers and move your legs around so that you can get in the most comfortable position possible.

Ensure that you have your TV off and any other lights dimmed. The only light should be a nightlight if you need to sleep with one. Other than that, there should be nothing that you see or hear. You should be completely at ease and ready to finally drift away for the night.

We are going to take you through a few positive affirmations that will help remind you that it is perfectly fine for you to fall asleep now. You can state these affirmations out loud if you'd like, but it's best to just let them flow through your mind so that you can get the peaceful sleep that you need.

The first thing you should remember is that

you are allowed to go to sleep and relax. There's nothing else in this moment that you have to focus on. The only thing that matters is that you are going to sleep right now.

You are allowed to feel peace and comfort, no matter what you might have experienced throughout the day. Now is the time where you can get the peaceful and restful sleep that you deserve.

Start first by noticing your breath. Count to five as you breathe in, count to five as you breathe out. We are going to do this with you now. The best method is to breathe in through your nose and out through a concentrated hole in your mouth.

Often throughout the day, we don't really notice our breathing, sometimes breathing alone can be the thing that gives you anxiety. Perhaps you are not breathing fast enough, or you're breathing too slow. Maybe you're not getting enough air and your body starts to get into a bit of a panic. Whenever you need to feel more relaxed, you can begin by using these methods. Now breathe in through your nose for one, two, three, four, and five. Breathe out through your mouth for one, two, three, four, and five.

We are going to count down now from 10. Make sure to breathe in for five and out for five. Once we reach one, you will be completely relaxed with your mind at ease. You will not think of anything and each time a thought passes into your mind, you are gently going to push it away.

Think of it like snowflakes falling through the sky. You could reach out and catch these thoughts if you wanted, but instead, you're just going to let them drop gently to the ground. Do not think about anything else other than sleep.

Breathe in now, and out. Breathe in, and out. Ten, nine, eight, seven, six, five, four, three, two, and one. You now see nothing in front of you. You are completely at ease and your mind is entirely calm.

You see nothing but black. You are totally restful and there are no distractions around.

The first affirmation that you are going to remind yourself of is that the only thing that matters now is that you sleep. You might be thinking of other anxious tasks that you didn't finish or what you might have to do tomorrow. Don't think of anything else other than sleep. These things will be waiting for you to get done later. You do not have to worry about them now. There is no point in thinking about what has to get done. The only thing that matters right now is sleep. Your top priority on your to-do list is to fall asleep. The number one thing that needs to get done before you do anything else, is that you need to get some rest. We all need to get the right amount of sleep so that we can feel better. How do you expect to go and perform well throughout your day if you are completely exhausted?

The only thing that you need to worry about in this second is just falling asleep. There is nothing else that is going to cause you any discomfort or worry. You are completely relaxed, and sleep is the only thing that matters. Sleep is one of life's greatest pleasures. We have to do nothing in this moment. Your job right now is to just sit there and close your eyes. You do not have to worry about anything that gives you anxiety or stress. Of course, these thoughts might pass into your mind, but as they do simply push them away. You know right now that the only thing to do is to sleep. That is the number one task.

If we do not do this, then we cannot do anything else the next day. If you are tired, then you will not be able to get the right thing done. Simply focus on your breathing and drifting away to sleep. Remind yourself, "I am allowed to sleep. I am allowed to be relaxed. I am allowed to be peaceful."

You do stuff all day long. You are constantly working, and your body is always tired. Give it a chance now to finally rest. It is not bad to get this type of sleep. You are completely allowed. You are valid. You are right and you are just moving on now. Remind yourself that the only thing that matters is that you focus on your breathing.

Even if you remember something that you forgot to do today, just let it go. These tasks will be waiting for you tomorrow, the tasks will never go away. But you still need to sleep in between.

Moving on, let's start to tap into our anxieties which keep us awake. Remind yourself now that "the things of the past, do not haunt me now."

What you might have done a day, 10 days, or 10 years ago, does not matter now. These thoughts running through your brain aren't going to provide you with any value. The anxious reminder of something embarrassing you did is not going to help you get your job done tomorrow. Running through these thoughts does not make them go away. Thinking about what you did over and over again doesn't make it any better. You are a new person now. You are allowed to move on from these anxious thoughts.

It's not always easy, and there will certainly be times where you can't do anything but think about something that causes you mental anguish. However, in this moment now it is okay to move on.

These things that you remember might have affected your life overall, but thinking about them as you're trying to fall asleep is only going to hurt you. You do not need to be constantly reminded of your regrets, your mistakes, or your embarrassing moments. Let your mind be at ease and push these thoughts out of your head.

The things that you did in the past and the experiences that you live through helped shape who you are today, but they don't have to affect what you do tomorrow.

You don't have to shut these thoughts out and punish yourself for thinking about them.

Simply let them gently pass through your head. No need to hold on to them for a long period of time.

They serve you no purpose anymore. Simply move on now and focus on falling asleep. Reliving past experiences can just cause you anxiety which is going to keep you up even later at night. You don't need anything that's going to keep you up. You only need things that are going to help you fall asleep.

The best thing that will help you fall asleep, is relaxing. Separate your emotions from the things that have already happened. Push these thoughts out of your head and move on. The next affirmation that we have to remind ourselves of is that you are not afraid of what tomorrow will bring.

Anything could happen in the world. You could go into work tomorrow and it plays out the exact same as it did before. You go into work tomorrow, and somebody could come in and ruin your day. Somebody could also come in and make your day amazing. Maybe the building gets shut down because of a really intense reason. Maybe the job that you have becomes obsolete. Maybe you walk in tomorrow and you get a $10,000 raise. Maybe you walk in tomorrow and you get a new boss and they instantly promote you. Anything could happen tomorrow.

Too often we focus on only bad things

happening, but remind yourself that good things could happen just as easily. Maybe the chance of something bad happening is higher in your line of work, but we have to remind ourselves that we can't predict the future. Even if you could get a glimpse of what the future is going to hold tomorrow, who is to say that we need to change it. Maybe changing the future is the very thing that causes it to be bad. In the end, you have to separate your thoughts and not let yourself play through scenarios over and over again of what potentially could happen tomorrow.

Anything is possible. Anything could happen. This is not to scare you. This is to simply remind you that there is no point in trying to predict what you might live through the day after today.

We are constantly struggling with anxiety because we play through the "what ifs" or the "maybes." This will happen too often, over and over again in our minds. This is not going to help you anymore. The only thing that you should be focusing on instead is making sure that you are centered on reality. Accept the fact that there are so many potentials of everything that could occur. Allow yourself to really visualize the things that are most likely to legitimately happen.

It might be easier to expect the worst, but this is not going to help you in the end.

Ensure that you are staying grounded in this moment and focused only on sleeping. Even if you do have everything planned out to a certain point tomorrow, there's always going to be a level of uncertainty that we can never remove.

There are plenty of freak accidents or random surprises that can throw everything off track. Don't let your emotions be glued to the "what if" of what could happen. Continue to focus on your breathing now and remember that you are in this moment. In this moment, the only thing that matters is that you sleep. Thinking of all the terrible possibilities of tomorrow is going to leave you lying in agony, just as thinking of the past can haunt you throughout the night. Let yourself free your mind from these constant terrified thoughts. You are a strong person who is going to be able to handle anything that comes your way tomorrow.

We no longer have to attach our thoughts and feelings to all of these scary unpredictabilities of the day-to-day schedule we find ourselves involved with. Be free with your thoughts and effortless with your emotions.

Feel light as you drift through these feelings and remind yourself that you are capable of handling anything that is going to happen.

Moving on to the next affirmation,

remember that you are feeling relaxed in your body.

Each point of tension through the top of your head to the tips of your toes is completely at ease now. You are not holding on to anything from the past. You are not afraid of anything in the future. You feel relaxation throughout every little corner of your body.

You allow air to come into your mind and out so effortlessly. You do not have to think about anything that causes you anxiety or mental anguish. You are focused only on this moment and making sure that you feel as good as possible. You are completely at peace, at ease, free and relaxed. Nothing is keeping your body feeling achy or sore. You are so light and effortless in everything that you feel.

The final thing that we need to remind ourselves of is that we are safe and protected.

Guided Meditation Therapy

Nothing bad is going to happen to us now.

We are in our own sanctuary within the very comfort of our bedroom. You are under the blankets, calm and peaceful.

Nothing bad is going to happen to you now.

You are completely taken care of, relaxed and at ease. You do not have to be afraid of anything happening.

Nobody is going to harm you. Nothing bad is going to happen.

The worst possible thing that can happen in this moment is that you do not allow yourself to fall asleep. Thinking of all the terrible things that could ever occur in the world right now is only going to make it difficult for you to actually get a good night's sleep. Allow yourself to be rested. Feel peace travel through your body. Let yourself sink deep into the bed.

Allow serenity into your nightly routine. The more relaxed you can be, and focused on happy and healthy sleep, the easier it is going to be for you to function throughout your day tomorrow. Remind yourself constantly that everything that you feel is completely normal. You are valid in your thoughts and emotions, and you do not have to worry about anything bad happening to you now.

These are all the things that you should remind yourself of every single night. Let's take you through them one more time. Remind yourself that the things that keep you up at night do not need your full attention.

The only thing that matters now is that you are going to sleep. Everything from the past does not matter. Everything from the future can be let go of. The things that have already happened do not haunt you now. You are not afraid of what tomorrow will bring. You feel relaxation throughout every corner of your body. You are safe and protected. You are content, peaceful and calm. All these thoughts and emotions can fill you with good feelings that will make it easier for you to fall asleep.

Remind yourself now that this is the most important task that you could possibly be doing. There is nothing else that you need to think of. There's nothing else that you need to do. Drift away so gently and easily, feel peace throughout every core of your body. Count your breath again now as we count down from 10. You will either be able to move on to the next meditation or just fall fast asleep.

Ten, nine, eight, seven, six, five, four, three, two, and one.

Chapter 2 – Overcoming Trauma, Anxiety, and Depression Meditation

Trauma, anxiety, and depression are all difficult things to have to deal with. If you experience one or more of these mental illnesses, then you know that it can be a struggle to get a restful night's sleep.

Anxious thoughts of your past or worries over what might happen tomorrow can really make it hard for you to stay relaxed all throughout the night. Even when you are sleeping, you might have constant nightmares that make it hard for you to feel comfortable in your own bed. In this meditation, we are going to take you through trauma. We are going to make it easier for you to be able to understand how to heal from some of these processes.

What you should know before getting into the meditation is that this is not going to be an instant cure. Mental illness doesn't go away with the snap of your fingers. It is a constant struggle to find the right mindset to overcome some of your biggest issues. This is a beginner exercise that is going to help unlock some parts of your brain needed to heal. There is a trigger warning for this meditation. We will be talking about wounds and trauma. If at any time your mind seems to wander somewhere dark and you don't understand how to pull yourself from this, feel free to stop and move and do something that distracts you.

Of course, the point of this meditation is going to make sure that you are calm and at peace, but we can't always help where our minds wander sometimes. If you get stuck in a panic, then remember to simply participate in more breathing exercises.

This meditation will help you heal and find the peace that you need to move on from some of your most challenging issues.

Make sure you are in a comfortable place because towards the end, we are going to encourage you to fall asleep. Keep an open mind and allow your thoughts to flow freely.

Meditation for Quieting Trauma, Depression, and Anxiety

After you have a physical wound on your body, there are four stages of healing that occur. These stages help to ensure that the wound doesn't get any worse and that it heals properly so that the rest of your body can still function. When we experience something traumatic or endure consistent depression and anxiety, it can be like a wound on your soul. These mental wounds don't have big ugly scars, like a scrape on your knee or cut on your face might. We have to remember, however, that these scars are still there.

These mental wounds are something that we still need to treat properly. In this meditation, we are going to help you understand how you can self-heal so that you can finally get the peace you need at night. Too often we lie awake thinking of the terrible things that we've experienced. How frequently do you find it almost impossible to actually get a restful night's sleep without waking up several times, playing a certain traumatic experience over and over again in your mind? You don't have to be a prisoner of your own experiences anymore. It is time to learn how you can best heal so that these wounds don't hurt.

Begin focusing on your breath right now. This is a great meditation to do before bed, but anytime that you need to be more relaxed, after dealing with trauma, anxiety, or depression is perfectly fine as well. Ensure that there are no distractions around you. You don't want any people, pets, music, sounds, sights, or anything else to keep you from being able to drift into a healthy and deep sleep. Feel as the air comes in and out of your body. Already, you can notice the way in which your body does what it can to ensure that you're getting taken care of properly. Even without us thinking about it, our bodies are constantly giving us the right things needed to survive.

We breathe, we digest, we live, we pump blood, and our heart beats. All of this continues to happen without us even having to think about it.

We do some of the work, but our body really comes in and does the rest. It knows exactly how to heal itself as well.

Think about this as you continue to breathe in and out. Breathe in through your nose and out through your mouth. This is a great way to keep you focused on your body. This is the method that you can use to ensure that you aren't thinking too hard about all that is negative for you.

Breathe in again, and out again. Breathe in through your nose for five, four, three, two, and one. Breathe out through your mouth for one, two, three, four, and five. Continue to breathe like this throughout the entire meditation.

When you get a cut or a scrape on your body, there are a few things that happen next in order to help you heal. The first step that happens after you cut yourself physically is that your body starts to go through hemostasis. This is the way that your body does what it can to stop the bleeding. At first, in this moment, your body is not concerned with healing. Your body is not going to immediately cover up that wound. All that matters is that the blood stops pouring out so that you don't have to lose any more of that.

This is incredibly powerful. This is what we do mentally. As soon as we experience something traumatic our bodies will try to stop it. It doesn't try to heal. It doesn't try to make sense of what's going on, and it doesn't try to give us a deep explanation to help further establish what we have been through. The only thing that our body does in this moment is try to make the trauma stop. It does whatever it can to make sure that we don't have to endure this pain anymore. Your body is incredibly powerful like this.

Understand what you might have gone through to make you try and stop the trauma. What experiences did you live through when your body did whatever it could to make this stop?

Did you try to self-sooth using outside sources? Maybe alcohol or drugs were able to stop the constant terror that ran through your mind.

Recognize this and remind yourself that whatever you have experienced is completely normal. This was your way your body tried to heal. We are past the stage now. Now it is time to move on to the next.

After you get a cut and the bleeding has stopped, what occurs next is inflammation. This inflammation is your body's way of fighting off any infection. It makes sure that the groundwork is in place for the actual restructuring of your skin to start.

Inflammation can be what occurs in us. This is when we are crying, when we are in pain, when we are screaming from anger, or when we are begging for things to stop. This is the stage that you might have gone through, but you are past this now. Your body was brave enough to pull you from this. You are so strong that you didn't have to deal with this anymore.

Your body did whatever it could to fight off this trauma and prevent it from happening again.

The point of this stage is to start a new growth process. You have moved past the initial fear and shock of what happened, and instead, you're looking for a way to heal. Unfortunately, not all of us understand the way that we are able to heal ourselves. This is when some things can get a little trickier. You are working through this now. You are fighting off this infection from ever coming back and taking over.

Next is proliferation. This is when the wound can start to close. Finally, it is not a sore spot anymore. This is the part that we need to focus on. You are focused on moving forward now. You understand that this wound is closing. It is finally healing. The skin is connected to itself once again to make sure that nothing can get in and nothing can get out.

Finally, in the stage of healing, your wound can form something new. This is when there might be a scar.

This is when you could be experiencing a reshaping of a physical part of your body. This is what happens to our soul. After we've experienced something traumatic, we never go back to the exact same way that things used to be. Instead, we only move forward and move on to something greater and better in the end.

Some people's wounds might heal incorrectly. They might let it become scar tissue on their soul, stopping another thing from functioning properly. You are not going to let this happen. You are healing now. You are feeling that wound finally close up. You don't have to let the feelings and emotions that you had at the time pour out anymore.

You're not closing things up so that you never deal with it again. You are simply closing it up because you are stronger and better now. You are moving past these challenging emotions. No longer do you have the challenging thoughts and feelings that used to pop up so frequently in the past.

The thing about scar tissue is that it will never be the same. Some scars will heal perfectly normally, and we don't even have to think about it. Then, there are plenty of other scars that can leave huge marks that can't be looked past. Eventually you'll get used to it. It is a part of you now, and this does not have to be so ugly. We don't have to consider scars as something scary or grotesque. They are simply another marking on our body. How many marks do you have simply from not even realizing that they are there?

Maybe there's a freckle on your cheek or a little cut on your arm from when you were a child and fell off your bike. Maybe you have some acne from when you were a teenager, struggling with the constant constellation of pimples across your face. Perhaps you can't grow hair on a certain patch on your body because of the scar. Maybe there's a big ugly lump on your leg that you hate to look at.

Whatever these are, we don't have to be afraid of them just like you don't have to fear the scar that is on your soul. You are moving on and past this now into a happier and healthier place. This scar is part of what makes you beautiful. Think of all the markings on a physical object that you see. Maybe you pull a little penny out of your change purse and notice all the small markings on this.

You can see all the scrapes and scratches along the face of the penny.

Each of these indicates something that it has gone through. It is a story; it is something that it came from. It is part of who it is. There is no going back or trying to erase it. This isn't going to help the wound heal. You have to let it heal properly to make it more manageable to handle later on.

Imagine just trying to cover up that wound. Imagine just putting makeup or a big Band-Aid over something that was infected. This is only going to make it worse. This isn't going to help you heal. Instead, the wound festers and it gets bigger and bigger.

Think about picking a scab and not being able to let it heal. This doesn't do it any good. It just makes it bigger and bigger and makes the scar deeper and deeper.

Let yourself heal naturally. You deserve to feel okay. What happened to you is not your fault. You don't have to hold on to these thoughts. We often remind ourselves of what we went through and this can make it hard to feel better. Make yourself feel good. Let yourself be happy. It's okay to experience good emotions even after constant years of feeling something so negative. Of course, it's not easy. Of course, this is not going to be a simple task.

This is something challenging. It is going to be a daily process that you have to work through, but it is going to be so worth it in the end. One day you will be able to look back on all of your struggles and your trauma and recognize that it has made you the person that you are today. You can grow and prosper from it. It does not have to be like a chain that keeps you strapped to the ground. You can spread your wings and be free. Feel yourself breathing in and out once again.

Breathe in good feelings and happiness. Breathe out the toxic negativity that has stuck around with you for so long. Remind yourself that with each breath you take, you are reminded at how alive and how strong and how brave you really are.

Each time you let air pass through your body, you are doing something good for it. You are taking care of yourself. You are loved. It doesn't matter who else loves you in this moment because you are loved by yourself and that is what is most important in the end.

You were brave and free. You are not tied just to the traumatic things that have happened to you. These are important because they can make up who you are. They give you a new perspective, and you have ideas that other people will never be able to experience. You understand evil and suffering on a different level.

You know what it feels like to hurt so much.

You recognize true pain, and not everyone will be able to say that. Of course, you might wish that you could be free from these experiences.

Perhaps you think about all the ways that you could become somebody who doesn't have to deal with challenging emotions. Maybe you envy those with easy carefree lives. Of course, that might be better, but we can never know. We will never understand because of our scars, and that is not a bad thing. These scars make us beautiful. They make us who we are. We can learn and grow and heal from them. They can teach us things. They remind us of what we've been through.

We recognize now that we are such an amazing person. These scars remind us of how resilient we are. They give us the recognition that we are able to take something so painful and grow from it. This scar does not destroy us. It is not the opening or the beginning of the end. It is the start of something new. It is a reminder that we will be better in the end because of this.

We know what true struggle is, and that means we recognize what real reward is. We have an appreciation for things like no other. We can have gratitude for the good because we have experienced so much bad.

Remind yourself of this. Recognize these emotions and let yourself relax. Let yourself be happy, free, calm, and collected. This is how you are going to heal. This is healthy for you. This is what you need.

Breathe in again and breathe out. Breathe in and breathe out. Feel the air travel so gently through your body. Let yourself heal and be happy.

As we count down from 20, remember to focus on your breathing.

Twenty, nineteen, eighteen, seventeen, sixteen, fifteen, fourteen, thirteen, twelve, eleven, ten, nine, eight, seven, six, five, four, three, two, and one.

It is okay to still hurt. It is okay to feel pain.

But you also need to relax.

We are now going to move on to a part where you can completely relax. When we reach one, you will have no thoughts passing through your mind.

We are going to help you drift deep into sleep now so that your traumas and triggers don't keep you up all night.

There is nothing but darkness around you. Now this does not make you scared, it simply reminds you of the significant life that you have.

You are a human being on this earth, and you are here as yourself. You are an individual, and you're strong. No matter what comes your way, you are going to be able to work through it. You have to get to sleep now so that you can perform as best as you can with all that you do.

It is okay to let yourself be relaxed. You do not have to be afraid anymore. Nothing is going to hurt you. No one is going to harm you. Nothing is going to scare you. You will not be haunted all night by the things that give you so much terror.

Count down now again. Let yourself get deeper and deeper into sleep.

Ten, nine, eight, seven, six, five, four, three, two, and one.

..... and you're closer and closer to sleep now.

Count again.

Ten, nine, eight, seven, six, five, four, three, two, and one, and you're closer and closer and closer to sleep.

One more time we are going to count down from twenty.

As we reach one, you will either drift off into sleep or move on to another meditation. You are safe, you are protected, you are healthy, and you are peaceful.

What happened to you in the past plays no role in this sleep now. All that matters is the moment. This moment is one where you can be completely relaxed.

You are not in any harm's way. You are at peace.

Twenty, nineteen, eighteen, seventeen, sixteen, fifteen, fourteen, thirteen, twelve, eleven, ten, nine, eight, seven, six, five, four, three, two, and one.

Chapter 3 – Meditation to Quiet Your Mind

Our brains are powerful tools that never seem to stop working.

They're constantly running through different ideas and other processes within our brain.

Throughout this meditation, we're going to help you find a more peaceful mind. This can be done through the use of a body scan. When you go through your entire body and notice how tension might be held, you can release it so that you feel better.

In the end, this meditation is a great one to do before taking a nap or going to bed at night. You will be able to completely calm down your body so that you can not only fall asleep easier but get a restful sleep that you won't get disturbed from all night.

Meditation for a Peaceful Mind

In order to have a peaceful and serene mind, you have to work through your body. What we don't always realize is how much tension we carry throughout each individual part of us. That anxiety or stress that you might feel which keeps you up at night doesn't just sit only within your brain.

It's something that travels throughout the rest of your body. You can hold tension and stress in places you didn't even realize.

If we really want to quiet your mind and be a more peaceful individual, than it's important that we understand how to relieve that tension within our bodies. This is going to be a body scan meditation that will guide you through how you can best release any tension in your body.

Most body scans will have you start with your

head, but we're going to do the opposite. Make sure that you are in a relaxed place with nothing around you. You should be completely at ease with zero distractions. Keep your legs gently stretched out in front of you and your arms placed by your side.

You can have parts of you slightly bent but nothing to where you're going to add extra strain or tension into that part of your body.

Let your feet hang loose and start to notice your breathing.

Breathe in through your nose and out through your mouth. This is going to be the best way that you can alleviate any feelings of tension within you.

Your breath will give you something to focus on that helps regulate the blood flow throughout your body. This sends good feelings all over you that can make it easier for you to start to relax your mind. It keeps each different part of you connected so that you can better find the needed peace within yourself.

As we count down from ten, breathe in for five and out for five. This is going to be the best method possible.

Remember to breathe in through your nose and out through your mouth. Breathe in now for five.

Twenty, nineteen, eighteen, seventeen, sixteen, fifteen, fourteen, thirteen, twelve, eleven, ten, nine, eight, seven, six, five, four, three, two, and one.

You now feel completely at ease. Each time a random thought pops into your head, gently push it out of your mind. No need to suppress it or ignore it as though it wasn't even there. Just simply don't pay it any extra mind. It's okay to acknowledge and notice it, but you don't have to let it consume your entire brain.

Keep your eyes closed in order to shut any other visual distractions out. You want to only be able to focus now on the air coming in and leaving your body.

Let's start first by noticing our toes. They seem so small and are a frequently forgotten part of your body. They have so much power. They help us walk around all day long. You can bend them as you please in order to release tension within the rest of your leg. You can pull them forward stiff, or you can pull them back towards you. Both of these methods help to stretch your legs in a way that releases tension. Curl your toes tensely for just a moment and then release. Take a few breaths and do this again. You can feel how much tension can be held into your toes. Your toes help guide you forward as you walk around, and without them, you'd be falling over a lot more often.

Though these little parts of our body seem so small, they carry so much weight at times. How often do you put yourself on your tippy-toes to try to reach something higher than you?

These toes have so much to them, yet we often forget about them. Let yourself feel peace pass into your toes, letting go of all tension. Breathe in peace and serenity and breathe out anxiety or stiffness. Move on now to the rest of your foot. This is like the stand in which you hold your entire body up. Without your feet, you wouldn't be able to properly hold yourself up.

These important parts of our body help carry us throughout our entire lives. They work in sync with our toes to take us places that we need to be. Your feet were once used as more of a signal for language. Think of our primal ancestors and the way that they can still hold or carry themselves just by their feet alone as they hop through different trees.

Your feet play an important role in your life, and they can have so much tension. Nothing feels better than putting them into a warm bath or getting a foot massage. Let yourself feel the tension as it releases itself through your feet.

Move on now up to your ankles as you breathe in peace and you breathe out stress. This is the way that you are going to be able to have a more peaceful mind. You might not think of releasing tension in your ankles, your feet, and your toes, as a stress relief method, but it is just the beginning of our journey throughout finding a more peaceful mind.

Move on now up to your calves. These are what connects your foot to your thigh. It helps make sure that your leg is complete and that you can walk around properly. Of course, people don't need their entire legs.

There are many other methods that help us move around.

But we still have to consider the way that the tension might be built within these parts of our bodies.

Notice now how you might hold so much tension in your calves. Maybe you barely bend them, or you keep them bent too much to the point that you frequently get cramps. Going forward around to the front of our leg is our shin. This all makes up the lower half of our leg and is vitally important to the way that we are able to move around in this life.

Let the tension in your shins and your calves release. Breathe in peace and breathe out any stress that might be held within this area. Move upwards now to your knees. These were what you used as your feet before you were able to walk. As babies, we crawl around the floor on our knees, making it easier for us to move. When we were once so curious about the world around us, our knees now help us to get lower. We can kneel for prayer or we can kneel while we simply bend over and work in the garden. We use our knees to get lower so we can reach for things underneath us, and we use our knees to help us stay comfortable when there's nothing else to sit on.

Your knees are important and make your legs more usable. You can bend your legs. Without your knees, you wouldn't be able to twist and move your legs so much. These make us flexible.

Move up now to your thighs. These are the big meaty parts of your legs. They will help make sure that you are able to strongly walk around as you wish. You use this part to help kick. It's what you sit on.

It's where you might be able to feel some tension that might travel up to your hips. This kind of stress isn't always noticeable.

We don't frequently think about carrying stress and tension within our legs. However, you can still have so much within these body parts and focusing on them makes it easier for you to let go of tension.

Move up now to your stomach. This is where you can also hold a lot of anxiety. We don't realize just how much our stomachs play a role in the feelings that we have, but it really is in charge of a lot. Your stomach is what processes all the nutrients and minerals that you give to it. It helps regulate your hormonal balance which will play directly into the way that you feel emotionally. Let yourself feel some of the tension as it is released through your stomach.

Sometimes we keep our abdomen stiff and filled with anxiety.

It's hard to think about certain things and you might get nervous butterflies which can be felt within your tummy.

Let yourself release the tension in your stomach. This is such an important part of our body that is the home to so many organs. We need to protect it and treat it as such. Let yourself feel as tension vanishes from your midsection.

On the opposite side is your lower back, this is another place that will hold an incredible amount of tension. Our backs are often mistreated as we are always slouching. What we don't understand is just how much it can be intertwined with our hips and our stomach and the way that we carry anxiety around with us.

Your lower back can be such a sensitive part as well. It holds your spine and so many nerves responsible for transmitting messages throughout your body. This is an important part that we have to take care of. Let yourself feel the tension leave your lower back. You can tense for a moment and then simply release as you regulate your breathing. When you tense your back, this helps remind you of just how much tension there might be.

Move up now to your chest. This is the place that holds your heart and your lungs - some of the most important parts of your body.

It's how the blood and the oxygen get regulated throughout the rest of your systems. It's an incredibly important part of your body and the place where we might feel stressed the most beyond just our minds. How often do you feel your heart race as you are nervous about something? Perhaps you experience frequent trouble breathing because you feel so stressed out.

These parts of your body are incredibly important because, without them, nothing else would be able to function.

Consider the way that you might feel stress

and anxiety within these parts of your body.

Do you feel sick to your stomach with a rapid heartbeat and quick breathing when you feel something that makes you nervous? Let yourself really feel your breath now. Focus on breathing in through your nose and out through your mouth once again, as we count down from ten.

Ten, nine, eight, seven, six, five, four, three, two, and one.

Feel as your heart continues to beat. Notice that it is getting slower and slower the more relaxed you are. Let's start with our hands as well. We can't overlook these important parts of our body. Your hands can hold whatever you want. They can pet your favorite animal, or you could cradle a little baby. Your hands help you write, create, draw, sketch and do anything else that you enjoy doing. You can craft something new, or you can fix a beloved object. You can write a friend a letter, or you can text them something meaningful. Your hands are incredibly powerful. We can't forget the way that we might even feel tension and anxiety within our phalanges.

Let your hands be flat against wherever they are now, whether they're on the bed beside you or you've placed them on top of your stomach.

Just simply stretch your fingers out and feel as the tension leaves them. You might not even realize how frequently you hold a fist with your hand. This fist is the ball of anxiety that we have to carry around with us. Keep your hand flat and open, and remind yourself that you are peaceful and you are calm. Nothing and nobody is going to hurt you within this moment. You are perfectly at ease, and you have nothing to worry about. Move on upwards to your elbows. Between your hand and your elbow is another important part of your body. This is what supports you when you might be carrying something.

This is the part of our body that we use to wrap around our friends and loved ones as we give them a hug. You can feel the tension within this part of your body.

Put your hand backward now, pointing your fingers towards your arm, and feel the muscle from your wrist to your elbow. So much tension can be held in this, but release it and continue to breathe as you allow yourself to become more relaxed, moving upwards to our biceps. All of this is where we are able to support the things that our hands do.

This is where we connect our hands to our mind. That's how we're able to transport messages and find support within these vital parts of our body. Feel the tension be released as you focus on this now. Continue to let the air come in and out of your body. Move up now to your shoulder and your neck. This is probably where you feel an immense amount of tension.

How many times has somebody touched your shoulder only to tell you that you are feeling pretty tense? This is an area that we need to focus on relieving tension from now, let your shoulders become more relaxed. Feel as your chest gets lighter and you can breathe just a bit easier.

Your neck has so many important muscles, and it protects what your nervous system needs to do and helps connect your brain to the rest of your body.

It's also where the hairs might rise on the back of our neck when you're feeling scared. You might feel fear and tension within your shoulders because you're always prepared. Release this tension now and let yourself really drop your head into the pillow beneath you.

Our heads are so heavy and we carry so much around with us, but you can feel that tension release and you now move up to your face in this moment. This is where you send so many signals to other people. You're able to smile, cry, grimace, or make other expressions that can sometimes comfort them.

You can show them that you love them and that you are happy whenever you want by using your face. It is where we eat and notice how we breathe. It is how we hear and how we see. Our face and our entire head is so incredibly important, too.

We have to feel the peace travel through this part as we transmit that message to the rest of our body. This is the control center.

This is where we need to ensure that we are releasing tension. Let yourself breathe in and out, in and out. You can do this body scan whenever you feel like you need to create a more peaceful mind. Continue to focus on the way that you might feel certain tension within parts of your body.

Release this tension as you notice it. As we countdown from 20, you will either drift off to sleep or move on to the next meditation.

Twenty, nineteen, eighteen, seventeen, sixteen, fifteen, fourteen, thirteen, twelve, eleven, ten, nine, eight, seven, six, five, four, three, two, one.

Chapter 4 – Meditation to Fall Asleep Instantly

This final meditation in this set is one that is going to help you fall asleep instantly. It is a quicker and shorter meditation that will take you through the visualization exercise.

This process makes it easier for your mindset to go from one where you might be thinking of specific things in your life to a place where you can get into a more dreamlike trance. You will be able to easily fall asleep and get that deep rest you need in order to conquer the day tomorrow. Again, ensure that you are in a comfortable place where you will be able to fall asleep for several hours at a time. This is best at night but if you plan on taking a rather long nap you could do this as well. Keep an open mind and focus on your breathing.

Meditation for a Deep and Quick Sleep

Sleep is incredibly important, but sometimes falling asleep can be difficult if we are not in the right mindset.

For this activity, we are going to take you through a visualization that will help ensure that you can get a deep sleep. It's important before falling asleep to relax your mind so that you can travel gently throughout your brain.

Start off by noticing your breath. Breathe in through your nose and out through your mouth. This is going to help calm you down so that you are able to breathe easier.

Begin by breathing in for five and out for five as we count down from twenty. Once we reach one, your mind will be completely clear. Each time a thought passes in, you will think of nothing. You will have nothing in your sight, and you will only think with your mind.

Make sure that you are in a comfortable place where you can sink into the space around you. Let your body become heavy as it falls into the bed. Keep your eyes closed and see nothing in front of you but darkness.

Each time a thought comes in, keep pushing it away. Breathe in through your nose and out through your mouth.

Remember to breathe in for five and out for five. Keep an empty mind and be ready to travel through a journey that will take you to a restful place.

Twenty, nineteen, eighteen, seventeen, sixteen, fifteen, fourteen, thirteen, twelve, eleven, ten, nine, eight, seven, six, five, four, three, two, and one.

You see nothing in front of you, it is

completely dark and you feel your body lifting gently up like a feather. You are light against the bed, and nothing is keeping you down. Continue to feel your body rise higher and higher. You are floating in space. There's black nothingness around you. You are gently drifting around.

You can see a few stars dotting the sky so far away, but for the most part, you see nothing. You feel yourself slowly moving through space. Your body is light and free, and nothing is keeping you strapped down. You're not afraid in this moment.

You are simply feeling easy and free. Breathe in and out, in and out.

You start to drift more towards a few planets, throughout your journey in space. You can really see now that you are up in the highest parts of the galaxy. You see out of the corner of your eye that you can actually catch a glimpse of Earth. You start gently floating towards it, having to put no effort in at all as your body is like a space rock floating through the stars.

Nothing is holding you down.

Nothing is violently pushing you either. Everything that you feel is a gentle and free emotion. You get closer and closer to Earth now and can see all the clouds that surround you. You start to move down, and you gently enter into the cloud area. Normally gravity would pull you down so fast, but right now you're just simply a gentle body drifting through the air. You get closer and closer to the land. You can see some birds here and there and a few cars and lights on the ground beneath you.

You pass all of this. Gently floating over a sleepy town.

Look down and let your mind explore what is it that you see down there. What is it that is in front of your eyes? What do you notice about this world around you as you continue to go closer and closer to home?

You are gently drifting throughout the sky. You can see trees beneath you. Now, if you reached your hand down, you'd even be able to gently feel a few leaves on the tops of the tallest trees. You don't do this now because you're just concerned with continuing to float through the sky. That's all that you really care about in this moment.

You're getting closer and closer and closer to home now, almost ready to fall asleep. You start to see that there is a lake.

You gently float down to the surface of the lake, and you land right in a boat. Your body is a little bit heavier now. You feel it relax into the bottom of the boat. Nothing around you is concerning you right now. You feel no stress or tension in any part of your body. You are simply floating through this space now.

The boat starts to gently drift on the lake. It is dark out now and you look up and see all the stars in the sky. All of this reminds you of the place that you were just a few moments ago. You start to drift closer and closer to sleep.

Do you feel as the tension leaves your body? You are peaceful throughout. You are not holding on to anything that causes you stress or anxiety. You are at ease in this moment. Everything feels good and you have no fear. You drift around in the water now for a little bit longer. You can see everything so clearly in this night sky. Just because it is dark does not mean that it's hard to see. The moon casts a beautiful glow over everything around you. You can feel the moon charging your skin. As you drift closer and closer to sleep, you feel almost nothing in your body now. You continue to focus on your breathing. You are safe, and you are at peace. You are calm, and you are relaxed. You feel incredible in this moment.

The boat starts to lift from the water. You feel as it gets higher above the water. You are even heavier now. Now you are completely glued to this comfortable surface as the boat starts to fly through the sky. You can look down and see that the city beneath you has drifted to sleep. You're getting closer and closer to home now. You can actually see your home beneath you. The boat gently takes you to your front door, and you float right in. No need to walk or climb stairs. You simply float in and straight to your bed.

You fall delicately into your bed with your head resting nicely on a pillow.

Here you are, in this moment, so peaceful and so relaxed. You are completely at ease. There's nothing that stresses you out or causes any anxiety or tension now. You are simply a body that is trying to fall asleep.

As we count down from 20, you will drift off to sleep. You will be in a very relaxed state where nothing stresses you out. You're not concerned with things that happened in the past, and you aren't going to stay up in fear of what might happen tomorrow, you are asleep. You are relaxed.

Breathe in and out. Breathe in and out.

Twenty, nineteen, eighteen, seventeen, sixteen, fifteen, fourteen, thirteen, twelve, eleven, ten, nine, eight, seven, six, five, four, three, two, and one.

Conclusion

These meditations are going to be an important part of a healthy sleep routine. In order to really alleviate your mind from any anxious thoughts or other things that keep you awake at night, you will want to ensure that you are calming down and becoming more relaxed before you go to bed. These meditations will be your key to becoming a happier and healthier person because of the consistent amount of rest that you'll be able to get.

The more that you practice these meditations, the easier it will be for you to get the restful sleep you deserve. You can also check out other meditations and series of books to find something with a more specific purpose, such as weight loss or positive thinking.

The key to a happy life is a happy mind and these meditations will do just that.

www.ingramcontent.com/pod-product-compliance
Lightning Source LLC
Chambersburg PA
CBHW060411080526
44583CB00012B/532